CASHING OUT
of Your
BUSINESS

Your Last Great Deal

Kathleen Richardson-Mauro
CFP, CBEC, CM&AA, CBI

Jane M. Johnson
CPA, CBEC, CM&AA

BOOK PUBLISHERS NETWORK

Book Publishers Network
P.O. Box 2256
Bothell • WA • 98041
Ph • 425-483-3040
www.bookpublishersnetwork.com

10 9 8 7 6 5 4 3 2 1

Printed in the United States of America

LCCN   2013941007
ISBN   9781937454852

Editor: Susan Malone
Proofreader: Julie Scandora
Cover design: Laura Zugzda
Interior design: Stephanie Martindale

DISCLAIMER

This book provides an introduction to business ownership transition planning. Neither the publisher or the authors have been engaged by the reader to render legal, accounting, tax, or other professional services or advice. Owners should engage competent professionals before making decisions related to the subject matter discussed in this publication. Neither the publisher or the authors shall have any liability or responsibility to any person or entity with respect to any loss or damage caused, or alleged to be caused, directly or indirectly by the information contained in this book.

The case studies in this book are based on actual client situations. Some names and identifying details have been changed to protect the privacy of individuals.

Contents

FOREWORD

When Jane Johnson and Kathleen Richardson-Mauro asked me to write the foreword to this book, I was honored. I have personally known both Jane and Kathleen for many years. We all share a similar passion for helping business owners achieve successful transitions from their businesses. With complementary talent and extensive professional backgrounds, they possess a unique ability and perspective, which you will experience in the pages of this book. As entrepreneurs themselves, coupled with first-hand knowledge gained from working closely with business owners for most of their careers, they bring a common-sense approach to a very complex issue—how owners may transition away from their privately held businesses, achieve their goals, and ensure business continuity at the same time.

When I started the MidMarket Alliance in 2005, we envisioned a world where private business owners would have access to the best client-centered advisors, along with the most relevant and comprehensive business information for good decision making. Since then, there has been a shift in the belief that the only way for a business owner to complete a business transition is to sell on the open market. Now, we commonly see many advanced transfer strategies.

As a seasoned dealmaker and the founder of the Alliance of Merger and Acquisition Advisors (AM&AA), I am keenly aware of the challenges business owners face in converting their many years of business ownership into the cash needed to fund their futures. In addition, I believe that if a majority of the many private ownership transitions are not successfully accomplished, it will result in a severe blow to our economy and may result in the single largest loss of accumulated personal wealth in our lifetimes.

This book could not have been written at a more critical time. The pending retirement of millions of baby boomers who are also business owners will create a tsunami of small- and medium-sized businesses that have to survive an ownership transition. If these businesses and their owners are not adequately prepared for this transition, their own personal wealth and millions of jobs could be lost. Business owners face many obstacles in making this change. And these challenges will likely increase with advancing age and as more businesses enter the marketplace. Against these odds, how can business owners successfully turn their illiquid business into needed cash? This very insightful new book will show them how.

Today, most financial advisory professionals focus on just one or two specialized services. Many fail to take into account the full picture, the owner's personal needs, and the company's overall performance and potential. Because the needs of the private business owner and the company are inextricably intertwined, superior financial advisory professionals, such as Jane and Kathleen, focus on the whole and not just the individual parts.

Jane and Kathleen are among the most highly valued business advisors, combining deep specialty know-how with broad generalist knowledge across many critical disciplines. They create extraordinary value by synergistically managing the delivery of all of the following advisory services:

- Assessment of personal needs and objectives
- Business valuation
- Strategic planning
- Business performance improvement and maximizing company value
- Corporate finance and merger and acquisition (M&A)
- Personal and estate planning

The need for transition planning is becoming more crucial every day. Finding a holistic and unbiased solution is the single-most important key to having a successful outcome. Most business owners will go through an ownership transition only once in their lifetime—they will have only one chance to get it right. No one plans to fail. Too many just fail to plan.

Whether you are thinking of transitioning next year or ten years from now, protect your hard-earned wealth and ensure the continuity of your business by reading *Cashing Out of Your Business*.

Michael R. Nall, CPA, CM&AA, CGMA
Founder and President
Alliance of Merger and Acquisition Advisors
Chicago, IL

Preface

Why It Matters

We are very passionate about business ownership-transition planning. Why wouldn't we be? Small businesses, those with fewer than five hundred employees, are responsible for nearly half of the GDP and employment in the United States.[1] They represent the very backbone of this country and what has made us uniquely different in the world economy. The dream of starting and owning their own business and providing a secure future for their families was the very desire that drove many people to immigrate to this country, enduring great hardships. Today, business owners still want to provide futures for their families. Their spirits, dreams, and tenacity keep our economy moving.

So, if privately held business owners *don't* have successful ownership transitions, our economy as a whole could suffer greatly. As their standard of living decreases and the jobs they provide are lost, we will take a huge economic hit, and the men and women who own these

---

1   Kathryn Kobe, "Small Business GDP: Update 2002–2010" (Washington, DC: SBA Office of Advocacy, 2012), http://www.sba.gov/sites/default/files/rs390tot_0.pdf.

businesses will not have enough money to comfortably live out the rest of their lives.

What about the wealth that will not be transferred to future generations? Do we really know what the cumulative effect of this could look like and how far reaching it could be? So much emphasis is placed on where the stock market is, what is happening in the housing market, what effect interest rates will have on our retirement accounts, but we don't hear much, if any, discussion on Wall Street or Main Street about the economic fallout we are facing due to failed business transitions. We owe it to our country and ourselves to do all that we can to ensure successful transitions.

There are millions of business owners who will need to transition the ownership of their business to others during the next decade in order to have financial stability for the rest of their lives. Some owners will desire to transfer their businesses internally to loyal management or family members while others may want or need to sell to an outside buyer in order to achieve their goals. A few owners will be able to afford to give away their businesses outright to others, but most will need to "cash out" in order to gain financial independence for the rest of their lives.

We decided to write this book because of our own experience with business-ownership transitions. We spent the better part of our careers learning how to start and grow businesses and working with business owner clients who were doing the same thing. But when it came time to exit, precious little advice was available. There was no "place" to learn about how to plan a successful transition. We had to experience it and learn from our mistakes. We knew a better way existed, and that drove us to seek education in this area and create a specialized advisory practice and this process for business-ownership transitions.

You have probably spent the best years of your life devoted to running and growing your business. You have invented new products and services, provided jobs, and shouldered all of the risk. You deserve to reap the rewards, and if you can do so *and* ensure that the business continues beyond you ... that will be true success!

Acknowledgements

First and foremost we want to thank our business owner clients who continue to demonstrate their incredible experience, knowledge and tenacity. Many of them are leaders in their industries and major employers and all of them took personal risks to build their businesses so that many others could benefit. We respect what you have built and we are grateful for your contributions to the economic well-being of this country.

Thanks to Lisë Stewart for inspiring us to write this book. Lisë's tireless passion and devotion as a business advocate takes her across our great country to speak with, teach, and listen to business owners who are trying to determine how they can ensure business continuity, preserve the jobs in their local community, and sustain family peace ... no small task! We consider ourselves fortunate to be members of her Galliard Group of family business advisors.

Special thanks to John Leonetti, president of Pinnacle Equity Solutions. John wrote one of the first books on business-ownership transition planning, *Exiting Your*

Business, Protecting Your Wealth. Pioneer, thought leader, and gifted teacher in the field of business-ownership transition planning, John trains and certifies advisors in the art and science of "exit planning." We are proud to say that we are Certified Business Exit Consultants and Pinnacle members.

Several other people assisted us in editing and launching this book. We will be eternally grateful to Sheryn Hara, Susan Malone, Marsha Friedman, Stephanie Martindale, Julie Scandora, and each of their team members for keeping us on track.

We are thankful that we were able to work together to write this book and deliver our message. Our purpose is to provide owners with an introduction to successful business-ownership transitions. Our hope is that owners will achieve all of their goals in the course of planning. And our wish is that they execute their very own "deal of a lifetime."

Introduction

What's Rockin' YOUR World?

If you are like millions of other baby-boomer business owners, you're beginning to think about life *after* your business. We are usually jolted into this mode of thinking by events that occur in our personal and/or business lives. These can be big or small, good or bad events … you never know what might give you the jolt.

For instance, birthdays that end in a 0 or 5 can hit us hard. The good news is that we made it. The bad news is we now feel old. And nothing makes us feel older than when that AARP membership card arrives in the mailbox. Are you still tearing those little white cards up upon arrival?

And how about the movies? When another James Bond film hits the theatres, we try not to think about how many have been released in our lifetimes and how many actors have come and gone in that role. The latest, *Skyfall*, really made us feel old … we won't say why in case you haven't seen it.

Many good events make us feel old as well. Our children graduate from college and get jobs (that's a really happy milestone); our children get married and begin having children and ask us what the grandkids should call us ... Nanny or Grammy, Grampy or Pop!

Our children or other family members join the business. This usually starts out as a good event, but their numbers can multiply quickly, and then trying to run the business gets more complex and challenging. This is where all sorts of family dynamics come into play.

Of course, bad events put our resolve to the test as well. Economic recessions force us to ratchet down the business and grow it back again. Although a cyclical occurrence in our economy, these can really sap your energy as you get older. "How many of these do I have to survive? I am *not* doing this again!" became the cry of many business owners as they were (and may still be) climbing back from the 2009 recession.

As a normal part of business, a key employee leaves your company, and you have to replace him. HR can be the most draining aspect of running a business. It's just not possible to keep *all* of your employees happy *all* of the time, although that looked so easy to do on day one.

Nothing makes you feel your own mortality like a health scare, the death of one or both parents, or the tragedy of losing a child. As if going from the on-deck circle to the batter's box, it triggers us to move on and get going with the rest of our lives.

And how about the other *D* word? The divorce rate for boomers is actually rising, and it is a life-changing event for sure. The divorce rate doubled between 1990 and 2009 among adults fifty and older in the United States (National Center for Family and Marriage Research 2012). This is often due to at least one partner going through a mid-life crisis, and it's not specific to boomer business owners—it's universal.

You may simply wake up one day, and you just don't *want* to go to the office. You feel weary, angry, bored, and/or unhappy, and the passion for the business is just not there any longer. You know it, and guess what, others have noticed as well! When you get to this point, your business usually begins to suffer. You may still feel passionate about your company, but events have rocked your world and jolted you into thinking about your legacy and the future of the business.

Several major questions now leap to mind:

～

Where do I start? This is complicated, and there are so many moving parts here. What about my financial future? How would my key employees react? What if my competition were to find out?

～

You're not alone. Throughout the chapters of this book, we'll discuss the essentials of successful ownership-transition planning so you can achieve your goals and live the life you now desire.

～

Is it selfish and irresponsible to think about my own legacy and my desire to work less or possibly leave the business altogether? After all, so many people are depending on me!

～

It would be selfish and irresponsible *not* to plan for this—you are not going to be here forever. Leaving a mess behind—estate taxes to pay, lost jobs, failed business—won't trigger kind thoughts about you or your legacy. Developing a plan will allow the business to continue in a financially secure way, whether you are there or not.

Often we hear sentiments such as this:

I still love my business and what I do ... is it possible to stay involved but simply transition the ownership ... you know, cash in just some of my chips?

Yes. And we will tell you how. The plan is vital.

A Business Ownership Transition Plan is a comprehensive written document that outlines how and when the ownership of a business will be transferred to others, either internally or externally, in order to achieve the owner's goals.

The rest of this book will discuss why you should start planning now and the steps to follow to create your own plan. These include:

- Determining your personal goals – "Getting Yourself Prepared"
- Calculating how much money you will need – "Counting Beans"

- Maximizing the value of your business – "Building a Better Box"
- Understanding your options – "Follow the Yellow Brick Road"
- Minimizing taxes and fees – "The Art of the Deal"
- Pulling it all together – "Paint by Numbers"

Every owner's plan will be unique to fit individual needs and situations.

~

There are a lot of moving parts, but with enough knowledge, you *can* achieve your goals and craft the life you want to live with proper planning and time. If you fail to plan, your future could be in jeopardy.

~

Chapter 1

Why Planning Now Is Vital

Simply put … you can affect the outcome if you have enough time! Doing ownership-transition planning in advance will significantly improve your chances of achieving your goals, providing for the orderly transfer of your business, and securing your financial future.

If you are like most owners, you have many pressing matters each and every day:

- Growing the business
- Staying ahead of the competition
- Recovering from the economic downturn
- Making good on promises made to your family and/or employees

You probably don't want to add transition planning to the list, but the consequences of not doing so are immense. Business owners who procrastinate about planning find themselves in precarious positions. Often their *only option* is to try to sell their business, and quickly, due to one of the dreaded life events mentioned in our Introduction.

⌒

On average, only 20 to 25 percent of businesses that put themselves up for sale
actually consummate a deal. Yikes.

⌒

And this statistic is only going to get worse! As more
and more baby boomers fail to plan and *need* to sell their
businesses, even greater numbers will be dumped on the
market, competing for the same buyers. If you and your
company are not prepared, you will not stand much of
a chance.

What would it mean to you and your family if you
were one of the 75 to 80 percent who can't sell? Is selling
to an insider an option for you? Will you be able to continue to live the life that you envisioned? Bad events don't
wait until you have time. They just happen. Then what?

Read on to learn what business-ownership transition
planning involves, and why it is so critical to achieving
your goals and securing your future.

Chapter 2

Getting Yourself Prepared

Now that we have talked about why and when to do this type of planning, let's discuss what ownership-transition planning involves. The first and most important aspect of this planning is getting yourself prepared.

This may surprise you, and you may be wondering why we are not talking about simply getting the business ready for sale.

Well, if you're like most owners, you have invested some (or most) of the best years of your life and most of your financial resources in your business. And you have taken precious little time off to reward yourself.

Once you started your business, your other passions likely fell off the radar, and now that you have been at it for several years, you are probably not used to thinking about yourself independent from the business.

~

Your identity and that of the business may now actually be one and the same.

~

It doesn't take long for this to happen. We have all made this mistake in the past. If someone had only cautioned us as we started down the business-owner path and then reminded us every so often along the way, maybe, just maybe, we could have avoided this. We could have led more balanced lives and kept our own identities in perspective. Now it will take quite some time to separate yourself—at least emotionally—from the business so you can begin to think about your situation objectively.

Goals & Objectives

As you begin to consider what a successful ownership transition looks like for you, you must first determine what you are trying to achieve … your goals and objectives. These will be both financial and non-financial in nature. Examples include:

Financial

- Receiving enough money to live on for the rest of your life
- Minimizing taxes
- Generating a nest egg that can be left to heirs or charity
- Creating a foundation that furthers a cause that is important to you

Non-financial

- Regaining balance in your life
- Following a passion that you gave up many years ago when you started your business

- Creating a legacy that will extend beyond your natural life
- Achieving and preserving family peace
- Taking care of loyal management and/or employees

Every owner's plan will be unique to his individual situation. This is very likely not *just* about the money for you, although this *is* probably the largest financial transaction of your life and possibly that of your extended family's.

～

This is about crafting the next and hopefully the *best* stage of your life. This is about remembering your true passions, determining what is most important to you, and what you *want* to do when you can spend less or no time with your business.

～

Getting yourself prepared is a process that takes time—another good reason to start this planning well in advance. Our lives are multi-faceted, and it is important to think about your goals and objectives for each area of your life. Your list may include goals in the following, as well as in other aspects not included here:

- Physical Health
- Intellectual Stimulation
- Recreational/Creative
- Spouse/Partner
- Family
- Residence
- Social Connections

- Spirituality/Faith
- Income-producing Work
- Volunteer/Philanthropic

©2013 Successful Transition Planning Institute, LLC.

Determining and understanding what you want to accomplish will re-energize you and provide you with direction as you figure out the best way to transition the ownership of your business to others. Once you have a clear vision, you will find the resources to accomplish it. It will give you an exciting new phase of life to step toward as you move away from your business. It will also enable you to minimize any chance for regrets, or seller's remorse, as it is sometimes called.

We have witnessed what can happen if owners never work on getting themselves prepared. In some cases, owners receive an offer for their businesses out of the blue, which is too good to turn down. They get excited about finally cashing in on all of their hard work, only to realize that once they have gone to the bank, they are bored, depressed and often end up divorced. How can this happen if they now have plenty of money?

They never took the time to separate themselves, emotionally, from the business, to explore their passions that had gone dormant so many years earlier, and to create identities and feelings of self-worth that were not tied to being a CEO. They never thought about how this next stage of life might play out. They never identified their hopes as well as their fears, never communicated those to their spouses, and never discussed how their relationships could be preserved and even enhanced with more time together.

Here is an owner who *thought* he was ready ...

Get Me Outa Here!

The owner of a successful business, in his early fifties, longed to be completely free from the day-to-day grind. He had started and run his business very successfully for twenty-plus years. He had grown to a robust company of twenty-five people.

He was tired—tired of employees, tired of fighting with contractors for payment, tired of being tired. He wanted to play more before he was too old. He was well diversified financially, and if you asked him what he intended to do with all of this soon-to-be-found free time, he would give you a list a mile long that included his beloved toys: race cars, air boats, fishing boats, etc.

Sound familiar? Well, maybe your list does not involve the same toys, but the desire to leave the grind and the exhaustion may ring a bell. Maybe you're sick and tired of being sick and tired?

He put his business up for sale, and after about a year on the market, a quality buyer was found, the deal was negotiated, and the big day arrived. Freedom at last, right? Well, maybe for the first month, but this story doesn't end there. You see, he already had all of the toys. He had been playing every weekend and actually had quite a bit of freedom. He was certain that this retirement would be just what he wanted and needed. How could it not be? No employees calling in sick, no warranty work, no bad debts, no payroll to make.

But, he was bored! His business was all he knew. He missed the employees, the customers, the challenge, the grind. He found himself stopping by to see everyone at lunch. He called his old buddies in the industry, but they were too busy to spend much time with him—they had their own businesses to run. He soon realized that the company had been his life. It was his family, his reason to get up every morning. After a twelve-month sale process and anxiously waiting for his freedom, he found himself wishing he could undo everything!

THE ACTUAL OUTCOMES

- This owner was not personally prepared. He had not separated himself from the business or found another cause where he could use his talents. His business was the framework for *who* he was. As the CEO, he was used to being in charge of everything, and now he was in charge of deciding which fishing hole he wanted to go to!

- His best friends were all still working.

- He now had a non-compete agreement that covered a very large area and prevented him from working in the only trade he knew.

- He felt lost and actually sold the home he loved and moved two hundred miles away to start the business all over again in the same industry.

- Over ten years have now passed, and he still owns his second company.

- Selling was not the right choice for this owner at this time; he wasn't ready.

THE DESIRED OUTCOMES

- If the owner had taken the time and had access to the right advisors and tools, he could have examined the areas of "pain" that needed to be addressed. He could have eliminated some of his day-to-day responsibilities and possibly changed his role in the company *without* selling, which would have provided him the needed relief *and* a succession plan when he was finally ready to call it quits.

- He would have had a thoughtful plan that took into consideration what he really wanted in his next phase of life and outlined options to achieve those goals and desires.

- He would still have the same company and his home, and he would not have had to move out of the area.

∽

The key lesson to be learned is to start preparing yourself now ... even if you are *potentially* years away from an official ownership transition.

∽

You never know when you might receive that unsolicited offer or what life events might just happen that will rock your world. Planning will improve your chances for a successful outcome and give you a lot more control over the process. Even though you may not realize how much your life revolves around your business, consider the potential impact on your social life, sense of accomplishment, need for challenge and belonging.

FEARS, CONCERNS, & OTHER BARRIERS

Along with determining your goals, it will be equally important for you to identify your fears and concerns related to this transition and the other barriers that prevent you from doing this type of planning. Many owners fear what comes next and worry about losing their life's purpose. Most wonder if they will have enough money to live the lifestyles they desire and what will happen to their employees.

Taking proactive action to address *your* fears and concerns, such as having a family meeting, discussing your plans for the future with your spouse, and identifying your actual financial needs, will allow you to find solutions and work through them so they don't hold you back. Facing your fears and concerns will provide clarity and allow you to move forward to determine your goals.

A wise man once said, "It is never too early to plan but may certainly be one day too late!" Don't wait until it is too late ... the stakes are too high!

Chapter 3

Counting Beans

In its simplest form, counting beans is about taking stock of how many assets you have saved *outside* the business, determining how much income you will need post-transition, and then calculating how much money you will need from the ownership transition. Very few owners are independently wealthy outside of their businesses. The vast majority will need to extract money from their companies to fund the rest of their lives.

Taking Stock

This is often an eye-opening exercise for the business owner. As we mentioned in our previous chapter, many owners have invested the majority of their money into their businesses. Many have also increased their spending (ratcheted up their lifestyles) to match the increasing profits of the company. This is often done, *at least in part,* to avoid paying taxes. But it is a dangerous game.

Talk about having all of your beans in one basket! Then next-generation family members get involved, and they put their beans in the same basket, and on and on it goes until the majority of the family wealth is all tied up in one illiquid, privately held business that isn't going to generate profits indefinitely. Yikes.

Despite being taught that diversification is the key to minimizing risk and generating the best possible returns, somehow owners believe that their businesses are their least risky investments because they control them. How many owners believed they controlled the performance and the future of their companies before the recent recession, only to find out that it simply wasn't true! They were forced to adjust down their lifestyles (drastically, in some cases) and/or go into debt. Some even lost their businesses!

All privately held companies are risky propositions, and the statistics exist as proof. According to the Bureau of Labor Statistics, approximately 26 percent of businesses survive fifteen years or more. Besides economic recessions, many other external forces can have dramatic impacts on these businesses, such as technological developments, health-care costs, and tax-law changes. It is not possible for you to completely control the business. *All* companies go through natural lifecycles and eventually go out of business. By being vigilant about changes and developments in your industry, you can adjust your business plan and reinvent the company as needed to stay competitive in your industry. Just think about the multitude of industries that have been dramatically impacted by technology and had to re-engineer their business models. Book and video stores, music, commercial printers, newspapers, telecommunications, etc., all come to mind, and there are countless others.

~

The fastest way to leave a legacy behind
is to lose the family fortune in the family
enterprise under your watch!

~

Unfortunately, that is not the legacy most owners have in mind. It is unlikely that other family members will step up to share the blame. Although they were eager to work for the family business and spend the profits during the good times, they probably never really considered how best to ensure its long-term survival.

Such was the case with this business owner ...

Not on My Watch

Sam was in real trouble. He had taken over the family business from his father a decade earlier, and the company had been in his family for over fifty years. Sam was the chosen member of the third generation to inherit the business, and he did not have to buy in or pay anything for his company stock—it was gifted to him. He did, however, agree to continue to pay his father a small salary throughout his retirement years to help him make ends meet.

The company had virtually no competitors. They had gone out of business or reinvented themselves ten to fifteen years earlier because times had changed and consumers no longer valued the type of products and services they were offering. The cost of doing business continued to rise, and the company lost money every year after Sam took over. Profitability had been going downhill for several years prior to Sam's arrival, and his father stepped away just as the company began to lose money.

Because of the long company history and family legacy, Sam could not bring himself to make significant changes to the business operations or its products and services. He felt compelled to keep the company the way it was to preserve the family legacy.

Sam had worked in another industry for several years before he took over the family business, and he had a large home, expensive cars, a country club membership, and kids in college. When the company began to lose money, Sam went to his bank, and they doubled his line of credit. When that was maxed out, he borrowed against his own home and put that money into the business. When that mortgage was tapped out, he borrowed more money, with his dad's permission, using the family real estate as collateral; the real estate that was supposed to be inherited by Sam and all of his siblings.

Sam's siblings were unaware of these developments. They thought everything was okay. After all, Sam didn't change his own lifestyle, and the business continued to operate as it had done in the past because Sam was funding salaries and regular operating losses with debt … a very dangerous game that usually doesn't end well.

Sam was paralyzed with fear and could not take action to save the company because it meant changing family traditions. He was worried about the company going down on his watch and what a terrible embarrassment it would be to the family who had lived in their town for over fifty years. But he just couldn't take action.

THE ACTUAL OUTCOMES

- Sam was in denial about where the company was in its lifecycle. There were no competitors for a reason—it didn't make sense to be in the industry. There was no longer money to be made on their products and services.

- Sam solicited the advice of different advisors over the years, but as soon as they suggested reinventing the company or closing the doors, he just couldn't take action, and he cut off his relationship with those advisors.

- The debt ultimately bankrupted Sam and the company, and the family lost its real estate, which had been pledged to the bank as collateral.

- Most of Sam's family stopped speaking to him because he had lost the family business, as well as their inheritance, and had given them no warning that the business was in real trouble. Sam never communicated it to them or asked for their input. Even Sam's dad was upset with him, though he was also guilty of putting his head in the sand and not taking any action before his tenure ended.

THE DESIRED OUTCOMES

- If Sam and his dad had stayed vigilant about changes in their industry, they might have been able to sell the company before it went downhill or reinvent it to stay in business.

- When the company began to lose money, Sam should have taken immediate action. The longer he waited, the more complex his situation became. He should have pursued a different and profitable business model or closed the company before the losses and debt mounted.

- Sam should have met with his father, reviewed the challenges facing the business, and discussed what needed to be done in order to avert a disastrous loss of family wealth. With or without his father's approval, Sam should have taken action to preserve the family's wealth.

- Sam didn't realize that the real legacy was not tied to the one family business that was gifted to him. The family and its *entrepreneurial spirit* were the real legacies, and good entrepreneurs always treat their businesses as investments, not as family heirlooms. To that end, they know when to start, grow, and most important, when to reinvent or get out of businesses before they lose money.

- Sam should have listened to the advisors who kept telling him he had to take action before it was too late.

DIVERSIFY YOUR HOLDINGS

Saving money outside the business provides diversification for you and more choices when it comes time to transitioning the ownership. For example, owners who have saved a lot may be able to afford to sell the company to family members or key employees who are unable to pay top dollar for the company.

This may be appealing if owners want to keep the business in the family or reward loyal employees who have made significant contributions *and* the business truly has future potential. A very small percentage of financially independent owners may actually be able to afford to gift the shares of their business to others, but most owners will need to get at least some money from the transition to fund their post-transition lifestyles.

DETERMINING INCOME NEEDS

In addition to taking stock of non-business assets, the other essential component to determining how much money will be needed from the transition is analyzing your current and post-transition personal-income needs. You may have a simple or very extravagant lifestyle, to which you have become accustomed, and you, no doubt, expect that lifestyle to continue beyond the company.

You may have sources of income besides your salary, bonus, and company-paid personal expenses. These might include real-estate rental income, interest, dividends, and eventually social security (you may *not* want to include this if you believe the system will be tapped out by the time you leave the business). If this is the case, you will need less money from the business-ownership transition than those who are highly dependent on their businesses. Regardless, knowing exactly how much you will need to live your desired lifestyle will be critical to accomplishing your goals.

CALCULATING THE WEALTH GAP

~

> The difference between what you currently have saved outside the business and how much you need to have outside the business to generate your desired income is known as the Wealth Gap. Most owners don't have an adequate nest egg and will be dependent on their business transition to fill this gap.

~

If you count your beans well in advance of any kind of transition, you can be proactive about saving more money and lessening your dependence on the business and the upcoming ownership transition. You can assess where the business is in its lifecycle (see our next chapter) and determine whether and how many family members should be involved at any one time. This analysis and proactive action can have a dramatic and positive impact on the family and its financial well-being.

CONTINGENCY PLANNING

We would be remiss not to mention in this chapter our belief that every owner, regardless of age, needs a contingency plan. As we will see in several of our case studies, premature death and the statistically more likely premature disability can have a tremendously negative impact on the business and the financial well-being of you and your family. Doing this analysis, determining how the business can continue without you, and securing the necessary insurance will enable you to avoid the financial disaster that these life events can cause.

How many owners think …

It's All Taken Care Of!

Famous last words, right? Well, unfortunately in this case, they truly were. This second-generation family business employed two grown sons (third generation) and many other employees. The father/owner, at age sixty-five, held the professional tradesmen licenses and had taken over the company from his dad thirty-five years prior. This business had provided for the family for many years and had a great reputation for quality work.

The owner's wife had been a stay-at-home mom and had never been involved in the business. Her husband was a great provider and took care of everything so she was in the dark about their personal financial situation. He didn't want to burden anyone with what he thought were his responsibilities. They both thought it was all taken care of. Then he was diagnosed with cancer, passed away, and the walls came crumbling down.

THE ACTUAL OUTCOMES

- The business was completely dependent on the owner, and he was the only one with the actual state licenses required to do this type of work.

- The owner was also the only one who could sign checks. Not even a durable power of attorney or other check-signing measures were in place to allow for the day-to-day activities of the business.

- No estate or contingency planning had been done. The husband, wife, and their two sons were all completely dependent on the income generated by the business.

- The business rapidly declined, and bills mounted while the owner was in and out of the hospital for treatments.

- The beneficiary of the owner's life insurance was the business instead of the wife, and the death benefit was far too small to keep the company afloat. Not knowing what else to do, the wife took a second mortgage on their home to partially pay business suppliers to keep the doors open. The wife almost lost her home due to the improper handling of these business debts. She eventually sold it and moved in with her brother due to lack of income.

- A second-generation company was dismantled—real estate sold off and the equipment purchased by a competitor for pennies on the dollar.

- The sons had to go to work for a competitor just to make ends meet.

The DESIRED Outcomes

- The owner wanted his sons to take over the business just as he had done from his dad.
- If the owner had worked on a transition plan and implemented even some basic steps, he most likely could have averted many, if not all, of these problems and the business would probably still be thriving today. He would have been able to:
  - Develop and implement a succession strategy for the sons to assume the leadership responsibilities over time. It takes years to groom others to take over.
  - Identify an internal transition strategy or sale to the children that would have allowed the owner's wife to continue to receive income from the business for the rest of her life.
  - Protect their home and other personal assets by purchasing enough life insurance. The home was sold to pay off the original mortgage and the second mortgage that was taken out on it to provide for the business cash-flow needs.
  - Secure his family's future and that of his employees through proper contingency, estate planning, and asset diversification.

ESTATE PLANNING & ASSET PROTECTION

Estate planning and asset protection are two additional subjects that we include in our Counting Beans analysis, but they are too involved to speak about at length in this book. We do, however, cover them in more depth in our workbook and owner-training materials. Learning more about both of these topics will allow you to protect your wealth and minimize the taxes that will be paid when the ownership of the business changes hands.

Most people think that having a will or a life insurance policy is sufficient estate planning. While this is a good start, it is certainly not sufficient. The same holds true when it comes to asset protection. Most believe it is taken care of by having liability protection and the customary insurance on cars, homes, etc. While insurance is important, it represents only part of what is needed to adequately protect your personal and business assets.

Asset protection and estate planning are necessary for the protection of your assets while living and upon your death. If not done correctly, your assets can be wiped out by unforeseen taxes, lawsuits, and many other unfortunate circumstances.

Chapter 4

Building a Better Box

In Chapter 3, "Counting Beans," we discussed how to calculate the Wealth Gap and how critical it is for you to diversify your holdings and save money outside of your privately held business. This keeps some of your proverbial beans out of the company and in other baskets, thereby reducing the risk of financial disaster and giving you more choices when it comes time to transitioning the ownership of your business to others.

We also discussed the inherent riskiness of all businesses, even if you make it past the first five years. In fact, business longevity often causes you to let your guard down due to a false sense of security of having made it this far. It can be hard to imagine that a business that has been around for lots of years can falter, but it happens all the time, and the decline can be dramatically fast.

Once a successful business model or formula is found, to simply rest on your laurels and get fat and happy is tempting. Profits are streaming in, lifestyles are really comfortable, and after a while, you stop watching competitors, stop attending industry events, and stop innovating altogether! Not a good scenario. Constantly remind yourself that the world is moving faster and faster. If you don't keep your head up and keep yourself hungry (at least in spirit), you may one day find yourself owning a company that *used* to be valuable and is now in serious trouble.

FINANCIAL DEPENDENCE ON THE BUSINESS

The reality is that most owners are financially dependent on their businesses and they will *have to* tap that value and take out money for their next phase of life, whether they stay involved in the business or not. We are all living longer, and most of us will need serious money in our later years to pay for living expenses and, more important, health or long-term care costs. We don't know any business owners who aspire to be living in low-cost housing or a nursing home paid for by the government until they check out. It's out of the question for most. We want to be able to afford to pay for our own personal care until the day we die so we can have it our way.

~

According to the "2012 MetLife Market Survey of Nursing Home, Assisted Living, Adult Day Services, and Home Care Costs," the average annual cost of nursing home care is between $80,000 and $90,000 and assisted living expenses average $40,000 + annually. We all know how much these costs continue to go up each year, so imagine what they will cost when you get to that age.

~

The sad truth is that without continued income from the business or from an income stream derived from selling the business, many business owners will see their standards of living dramatically decline.

The only logical thing to do, therefore, is to remain vigilant and nurture the company to maximize and protect the value all along the way. Always treat the business as an investment, not a lifestyle. And again, avoid the trap of letting your personal identity get wrapped up in the company. By staying vigilant and clear, you will know when to reinvent your business and when to sell (either internally or externally) so you can tap into the value, realize your gain, and get enough money to achieve your goals! In order to do this, it is important, first, to understand how businesses are valued and what drives their value.

BEAUTY IS IN THE EYE OF THE BUYER

Business valuation is a complex topic, and the professional advisors who prepare business valuations go through comprehensive training and testing to achieve their certifications. Our goal in this book is to provide business owners with a high-level overview and introduction to some of the related terminology that is used in the profession. We always recommend that owners engage with advisors who are well versed in this field in order to truly understand what their business may be worth.

Publicly held companies have a definitive value, on any given day, based on their stock price. By contrast, privately held companies have a *range of values* on any given day. Value or "beauty" is ultimately assigned by prospective buyers based on their perception of your business. Buyers want your business to be profitable, of course, but they also want it to be a quality one; by that, we mean a well-run business with great potential. Yes, this is a subjective process, based on lots of factors that aren't entirely financial in nature.

What do we mean by "quality" and "well run"? Buyers consider many, many factors when they evaluate a company, but first and foremost, they want to know that the business is not dependent on you personally. That is, they want assurance it can be run successfully in your absence by your terrific management team or key employees. They want to hear about your obsession with customer service and retention, quality of product and services, processes and procedures. They want to see your strategic business plan and learn about the company's potential for future growth and earnings. They want to know that you are well respected in the industry and your competitors take you seriously. And to top it off, they want you to demonstrate that very little risk exists to owning your business. They need to feel warm and fuzzy if they are going to invest in your company.

The list of criteria for being a quality company goes on and on. Trust us when we tell you that potential buyers will leave no stone unturned as they evaluate you and your company through a process known as due diligence. Here are eight of the most important characteristics or "value drivers" that prospective buyers look for in their acquisition candidates:

Key Value Drivers
Increasing Revenue & Profits
Growth Potential
Clean Financials
Solid Management Team
Quality Products & Services
Strong Sales & Marketing
Low Risk
Systems & Processes in Place

If you make it through the "sniff test" and get to the offer stage, the purchase price will often be stated as a multiple of normalized earnings (often referred to as "Adjusted EBITDA" or Earnings Before Interest, Taxes, Depreciation, and Amortization). The process for normalizing your earnings usually involves starting with your reported internal earnings and adding back one-time, non-recurring expenses, i.e., moving expenses as well as your excess compensation and personal expenses that may be on the company books—club memberships, vacations, payroll expenses for absent family members ... you get the idea.

The goal is to determine what someone "off the street" could earn if he bought your business. Normalized earnings is then subjected to a multiple, based on the buyer's perceived risk and desired rate of return, to arrive at a purchase price or value for your business. Multiples can vary widely across different industries and by company size (larger companies command higher multiples, typically). They also vary with market conditions … they go down during buyers' markets and up in sellers' markets. It is not uncommon to see multiples as low as one, or as high as five for smaller Main Street and lower middle-market businesses. Certain types of buyers may pay a much higher multiple, given the right circumstances. We discuss different types of buyers in our future chapters: "Follow the Yellow Brick Road" and "The Art of the Deal."

~

The bottom line is that buyers will apply higher multiples to quality companies. If you work hard to improve your business, buyers will be willing to pay more for it. Due to the multiple effect, every dollar you add to earnings will come back to you many times over in the purchase price. Now we are getting somewhere. Planning in advance will give you time to improve your business and maximize its value.

~

Unfortunately that is *not* what this owner did …

Living the Lifestyle!

This story is about a very successful family business that had been around for more than twenty-five years. Some long-term employees were just like family. The owners, a husband and wife, had a grown son and a son-in-law working in the business. All three families were dependent on this company for not only a sizeable income but also health insurance, vacations, travel, and many other perks. This company was operated as a C corporation and all of its assets, including substantial real estate, were held inside the one corporate entity.

The sixty-five-year-old owner wanted to realize the rewards from his business by selling to a third party. Unfortunately, he was not willing to stop living out of the business in order to demonstrate the actual profitability of the company to the buyer, even though each dollar he consumed would have translated into approximately five dollars at the time of a sale. His main objective was based on short-term thinking: "I don't want to pay more in taxes!"

In addition, neither he nor his family members had ever saved any substantial money outside of the business. They only consumed! And to top it off, the business owner *was* the business. Even though his son and son-in-law were very capable, he was not ready to let go of the reins, and he continued to restrict their involvement. After all, they just "weren't ready."

Unfortunately this attitude is far too common among owners.

The sad outcome here is that a buyer was found and a price was negotiated but nothing was ever going to enable this owner to let go of this business that provided his lifestyle and his position of control. Once he realized that the buyer was not going to purchase his C corporation stock due to the possibility of inherent liabilities and he was going to have to face double taxation on the asset sale, things quickly deteriorated. The owner wanted to increase the sales price to make up the difference. In other words, he wanted the buyer to pay his tax bill. Otherwise, he would not receive enough money to maintain his lifestyle for more than a few years after all of the taxes and fees were paid.

The added tragedy was that his current advisors were either not capable or were unwilling to assist him with this minefield. Rather than plan ahead and prepare for the impending tax issues or counsel him about internal transfer possibilities, they focused unrealistically on demanding that the buyer purchase the stock when the vast majority of all business transactions are asset sales.

Another long-term advisor, the family estate attorney, was brought in to draft the proposed purchase documents on the *buyer's* behalf, believe it or not. This was a multi-million dollar transaction, and he drafted a real estate contract! The owner mistakenly believed that this advisor was watching his back. At this point, the highly qualified buyer marched right out the door with his multi-million dollar cash offer, and the business continues today with no succession or contingency planning, a looming estate-tax issue, and huge transfer issues, not to mention all of their future incomes in jeopardy.

THE ACTUAL OUTCOMES

- The owner was not personally or financially prepared to move on.

- There was no diversification of assets or other income-producing activities. The owner and his immediate family had all ratcheted up their lifestyles, and they were very dependent on this business to provide continuing income.

- The owner was not running the company as an investment but as a means for his lifestyle by minimizing profits to minimize taxes. This decreased the value of the business since the profits were substantially less than they could have been. Assuming a multiple of five, this meant that every dollar of profit that went unreported resulted in a five-dollar loss in selling price.

- This owner received insufficient and, in some cases, incorrect advice from his advisors. If his advisors had taken the time and had been qualified to help him ascertain his true goals and objectives, they would have found that this owner really wanted his business to go to his family. He did not want to put the company in debt or be the bank himself, which would have enabled them to buy him out, but other strategies could have been used to accomplish his goals and secure his retirement and the future of his family. No one took the time or had the ability to ask him the truly important questions and offer comprehensive integrated solutions. Many advisors are ill-equipped in these areas.

- The dreaded C corporation strikes again. This entity structure was commonly used many years ago, and other than some write-offs that it provides for owner benefits, there are few, if any, reasons for its use. In fact, the double taxation triggered on an asset sale of a C corporation is extremely costly (the corporation pays tax first, and then the owner pays tax again on the net proceeds). The solution provided by his advisors was to require the buyer to purchase the stock of his company. Most buyers' attorneys will advise against such a transaction unless it comes with a substantial price discount and very stringent guarantees that keep the seller liable for years to come.

- Clearly no asset protection strategies were put in place since the business and real estate were in the same entity.

- The owner did not have a plan for the continuance of the business if something were to happen to him. No one had the access or the ability to sign checks if he was incapacitated.

- The advisors were not working together and were not qualified to counsel him in a transaction of this magnitude. They had been his advisors for many years, and the complexity and nature of his business outgrew them. Unfortunately, business owners develop very strong loyalties to their advisors and often feel compelled to continue with them and don't recognize when they are not capable of handling these types of situations.

- This business may end up as another dismal statistic of a family-held, profitable business that will close its doors upon the death or disability of the owner or sell to a competitor at a fraction of the true value. The family is under the false assumption that their lives will continue on without interruption or dramatic change.

The DESIRED Outcomes

Had this owner engaged in the transition planning process in a timely fashion, he could have:

- diversified his holdings through some tax-advantaged savings strategies, thereby reducing taxes and saving outside of the business.

- created adequate contingency and succession plans.

- explored and chosen his best transfer options since his true desire was to see the business continue for his family and his employees.

- elected to change the C corporation to a different entity type to avoid the double taxation.

- separated his real estate from his business assets to better protect them and give himself more options at the time of the transition.

- minimized his transfer taxes and fees even without a third-party buyer. Selling externally is usually the most expensive option when it comes to taxes and fees.

- relinquished control over time, and his retirement and lifestyle would have been secured. He could have even remained involved, but in a different capacity.

- assembled a team of advisors that were well versed in ownership-transition planning to work together to achieve his goals.

Chapter 5

Follow the Yellow Brick Road

In the previous chapters, you learned why getting yourself ready, counting your beans (determining your financial needs), and maximizing your business value is critical to preparing for an ownership transition. As this chapter title would imply, we ask you to follow this *road* in order to explore your transition options and their suitability for your particular situation.

TYPES OF BUSINESS TRANSFERS

There are two general categories of business transfers—internal and external. "Internal" refers to selling or gifting the business to an insider, such as key employees, managers, or a family member involved in the business. "External" refers to selling to an outsider, such as a competitor, customer, or investor.

Building on what we discussed in our last chapter, it is important to understand that different transfer options have different transfer values, as well as different fees and taxes. Pros and cons exist to each type of transfer, and assessing the different options for suitability or how they will either accomplish or not accomplish your financial and non-financial goals is a crucial step in planning your transition.

Contrary to what most business owners believe, usually several transfer options are available to them *if* they plan ahead. Yes, that word again. You see, the less time you give yourself to plan the transition from your business, the fewer options you will have.

NON-FINANCIAL CONSIDERATIONS

Even though the financial considerations of an option will factor heavily into your decisions, don't underestimate the importance of weighing the non-financial aspects of each transfer option as well. Give ample consideration to the very important topics we covered in the chapter "Getting Yourself Prepared."

What are your personal post-transition plans? What do you really want to accomplish with this transition? How will each transition option impact and affect employees, family (involved and not involved in the business), customers, community, and your legacy? What matters most to you? These questions can be answered only by you.

SELLING YOUR BUSINESS TO AN OUTSIDER

So what is the right option for you? Most owners think of selling their businesses to an outsider as being the only option available. This is just one option, and as we learned in Chapter 2, the odds of completing an external transfer are actually against you. It can also be the most costly transfer method in terms of taxes and advisory fees. If you *are* successful, it will likely result in the highest *gross* dollar amount for the business, but it may or may not *net* you the most money without proper planning. Too many times, owners are tempted by that big payday, only to find out the big payday was for everyone *but* them. The IRS and the advisors involved had a good day, but the business owner may feel cheated for all of his years of hard work. These fees and taxes can be mitigated, to some extent, through proper planning. But it takes *time*.

You may determine that this type of transfer suits you best if you found out in "Counting Beans" that you are highly dependent on your company to satisfy your post-exit financial needs. However, this may be accomplished only by planning ahead and finding a *strategic* buyer who will pay top dollar for your business.

Sadly, selling externally may be your *only option* if you fail to plan and don't have anyone internally who can buy your business. Unfortunately, selling as a last resort is often akin to having a fire sale for your business or getting pennies on the dollar. This, along with shutting the doors and simply liquidating, is the default transition option for those who leave their futures to be determined by death, disability, or some other catastrophic event.

According to a study published by the Life Insurance Management Research Association (LIMRA) in 2008, 40 percent of businesses are forced into liquidation because they haven't taken actions for succession or exit, and this is prior to the baby-boomer business-owner transitions!

If selling to an outsider is your desired method of transfer, planning will enable you to make this option work *for* you instead of against you. Knowing what and how you need to prepare can greatly improve your chances of being one of the five businesses that sells and for top dollar! We discussed how to prepare your company in the chapter "Building a Better Box," and we will talk more about how to achieve this goal in our next chapter, "The Art of the Deal."

Selling Your Business to an Insider

So, what about internal transfer options? These require planning and preparation as well. They have names like management buyout (MBO), leveraged buyout (LBO, which is an MBO with debt financing), and employee stock ownership plan (ESOP). These options will often require third-party (i.e., bank) debt and may also require you, as the owner, to participate as a lender. For the most part, these types of transfers will result in a *smaller* gross dollar value for the company than the external sale but could actually result in a *greater* net dollar amount due to the minimization of taxes and fees.

Many tax advantages exist to some of these internal transfer methods, especially the ESOP. These types of transfers are too often considered as being only for the largest companies. This can be a costly false assumption. They may actually provide some of your best strategies to accomplish your goals. Here is a perfect example …

Which Option Should I Pick?

Having options is always nice. Choices broaden our opportunities. But they can also confound us immensely. We don't want to live in a chocolate-and-vanilla world, but we can stand in front of the ice cream counter at Baskin-Robbins and stare at sixty-six flavors for ten minutes and still pick our one favorite.

A very successful second-generation company had grown immensely, and the CEO, now in her sixties, wanted to retire as her dad had done many years earlier. When she had come into the company over thirty-five years ago, they had been doing a little over three million dollars in sales, and now, under her guidance and efforts, the company had quadrupled in size.

This was a different ball game. Things were much more complex now. She had a very solid management team, so the continuation of the company was not an issue, and the future looked bright as well. She had done a good job of building a valuable "box." The question was ... should she sell it? What would happen to her long-term employees if she did? They all had families and had been very loyal. What would she pay in taxes and fees? She was a C corporation, after all, and she knew that potentially meant double taxation, but she had never done anything about it. If she sold to management, what would that mean? Would that provide enough income to support her family's lifestyle and future needs? So many choices ...

The owner had done pretty well at diversifying her holdings by saving money outside the business, but she still knew that the bulk of her wealth was in this business. How could she get it out? She knew that alternatives had to exist, but the more she spoke to her attorney, her CPA, and her friends who had already sold or retired, she just became more confused and concerned. Time was ticking along, and she wanted to be able to turn over the reins and enjoy her retirement. She was ready, but how should it be done?

The last conversation she had with her CPA scared her the most. They were just talking about ball park numbers if she were to sell the company for what they both thought it was worth, and the taxes and fees were staggering. All of those years her dad had labored and the twenty-five years she had struggled on her own after her dad retired would be vaporized to a large extent by her mandatory contribution to the IRS and the advisors. Where was the justice?

She put this idea of leaving on the back burner. After all, she really didn't know which way to go. But time moves quickly. Then her health started to fail. The doctors told her that she needed to slow way down if she wanted to see her seventieth birthday. So now the decision had to be made; she could not delay anymore.

The advice she was given by her CPA and attorney was to consider a LBO, or leveraged management buyout. They felt it would probably be the best move and would provide the lump sum that the owner needed to secure her future and meet her needs. She knew the company was solid and could take on the necessary third-party debt, which would not overburden the new ownership team. It all made sense, and frankly, she was tired of exploring options. She surely had considered them all and needed to pick one.

Well, she put this in motion and sold to her loyal team. Yes, it was a good feeling to be finally free, and it made her doctors happy, but she still had a really tough time accepting the taxes, which took a huge bite out of her proceeds from the sale. At least she didn't have to pay fees to a broker as well.

The ACTUAL Outcomes

- The seller did not have a comprehensive and written plan to achieve her goals and assess her different options. Other options actually *did* exist that she didn't even know about or consider.

- The lack of tax and entity planning and her choice of a less than optimal transfer option cost her millions in unnecessary taxes.

- She did not have the correct advisory team to assist her in this process. They were not experienced in the transition planning process and were not well versed in these types of strategies, so the owner was left to make decisions without proper guidance and information.

- Loss of additional generational wealth. Her family, other heirs, and/or charitable causes will not benefit from the additional money that could have been captured through proper planning.

THE DESIRED OUTCOMES

- If the seller had developed a comprehensive transition plan to achieve her goals, she would have discovered that one of her best options might have been the ESOP. This would have provided the continuity of ownership for the company, security for her management team, a lump sum to fund her retirement, and most of all, *huge* tax savings. Advanced strategies such as these require specialized advisors, and she could have benefited greatly from their expertise in these areas.

- She would have saved approximately two million dollars in federal and state taxes. Not a small number for a little planning!

BUILDING A SUSTAINABLE COMPANY

As we discussed in "Building a Better Box," the business cannot be dependent on *you*. It not only diminishes the business value but also creates a situation where it becomes almost impossible to accomplish most transfers successfully.

One of the most difficult things for any owner is relinquishing control. For the most part, business owners are extremely "in control" people. They usually have similar personality traits that have enabled them to be very successful. They are typically driven, type A personalities who thrive on challenges. They are leaders and doers, not followers. They are risk takers, putting it all on the line every day. This is probably how you built your successful business, and you should be proud of your accomplishments.

These same traits, however, can be a handicap during the transition from your business. You will need an empowered, capable management team to run the company, whether you choose an internal or external transfer. This means you will need to delegate and relinquish some control, as well as learn to rely on and trust others.

This may be uncharted territory for you since most decisions and problem solving rest solely on your shoulders today, fostering your belief that you are in control. But as we discussed, control is an illusion. Are any of us *really* in control? Herein lies the lurking time bomb. If you are one of the owners who is always in control, what happens to the business and the business value if (and when) something happens to you? Building a true team not only prepares you for a smoother transition but is also critical in developing a good contingency plan. None of us will be here forever. An eventual transition is inevitable.

As we discussed in "Getting Yourself Prepared," your relationship with your business will most likely need to be redefined. This takes time. Any transition option will require adjustments, at least to some degree. One of the greatest achievements an owner can accomplish is the transfer of that leadership role. This is what true succession is all about. No transfer can happen without it. The only transition option that does not rely on these principles is liquidation. Don't let this happen to you.

⌣

In summary, if you allow enough time and plan ahead, you will probably have several transition options. Conversely, the less planning and the less time you have, the fewer your options. Don't leave your future to chance. Start the planning process now, even if you do not wish to leave your business for five or ten years. A solid transition plan will allow you to positively impact the outcome as much as possible. Be proactive and don't procrastinate!

~

Read on to learn more about marketplace dynamics, the minefield we call the selling process, and how to get the most out of your transition.

Chapter 6

The Art of the Deal

If you believe that your best transition option may be to sell externally, or you are strongly considering it, you are not alone. As we mentioned before, this is the option most often attempted, but not often achieved. Some owners attempt it because they don't know about other options. Some believe it will net them the highest dollar amount. And others simply do not desire an internal transfer or just don't have anyone internally who could buy it. We hope this has not become your only option. Chances are, if you are reading this, you still have time.

In considering an external transfer, understanding the marketplace will help you achieve the best possible results. Don't be fooled into thinking this is a simple process or will take only a few months. Do not travel down this path alone and without planning!

BUSINESS TRANSFER MARKETPLACE

We call this discussion about the transfer process "the art of the deal" for good reason.

～

The art is in positioning your business in the
best possible light, finding the right buyer,
and negotiating the best possible deal.

～

Since your business is not a publicly traded company,
like IBM or Cisco, you do not have a ready market for
your business. No one can look up your share price on
a stock exchange to determine the purchase price. That
would be too simple.

The marketplace for private-company transfers is currently a buyer's market, but it is fragmented and does not
have ready access to needed credit. There is a tremendous
amount of money on the sidelines, in banks, private equity
firms, other companies, and yes, even held by individual
investors. The key question is, therefore—*how* do you get
them to spend it on *you* and pay top dollar?

This illustration depicts the selling cycles of privately
held businesses for the last thirty years:

Ten Year Transfer Cycle

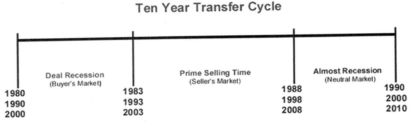

Source: Robert T. Slee: *Private Capital Markets*

This shows, historically, when it has been a buyer's
market, a seller's market, and a neutral market during
each of the last three decades. If selling to an outsider is
your strategy, you would, of course, want to sell during

a seller's market so you can maximize the price. The future is uncertain, but if history repeats itself, the next prime selling time for privately held businesses will be 2013 to 2018.

As of this writing, market activity is definitely picking up. According to the fourth quarter 2012 *Market Pulse Survey Report* published by the International Business Brokers Association (IBBA) and M&A Source, for the first time, baby-boomer retirement is the number-one reason driving business sales across both the Main Street (businesses up to two million dollars in value) and lower middle-market sectors (businesses from two million to fifty million dollars in value).

~

The onslaught of businesses going to market is likely to pick up and continue for the next ten to fifteen years due to the baby boomers hitting retirement age or experiencing a life event, such as death, disability, or illness.

~

What happens when you have an oversupply? Right, values drop. Think of the current real estate market. During the early to mid-2000s, the United States experienced an overinflated real-estate market in most parts of the country. When the bubble burst and the bottom fell out, the ensuing bust nearly collapsed the market in many metropolitan areas. We now have an oversupply of homes, some distressed, others not, and this means that sellers cannot command the highest price unless they have something very unique to offer. Sale prices have dropped, and credit is harder to get. So what happens if a flood of small businesses hits the market, some distressed, some not? The same rules apply. Be prepared, equipped, and "dressed" for success in order to stand out from the crowd!

~

This is why we say that business owners cannot simply pick an age at which they want to sell or retire. They have to be cognizant of the business-transfer cycles and the anticipated impact of things such as this baby-boomer demographic when they think about the right timing for their situations.

~

As we have mentioned several times, the US Chamber of Commerce and many business-broker associations publish statistics on how many businesses successfully sell, out of those that attempt it, and the recent average is approximately one in five, or 20 percent. Surprising indeed! And these are the statistics *before* the pending onslaught of businesses preparing to hit the market. The dissipation of personal wealth due to the inability to turn privately held family businesses into liquid assets (cash) will dramatically alter owner retirements and negatively impact future generations.

~

In the last four years, many business owners have experienced a devaluation of their assets outside the business as well as a loss of wealth inside their businesses due to the recent economic recession. Millions of owners will not have enough money for the rest of their lives if they can't achieve a successful ownership transition.

~

How to Navigate in the Marketplace

In order to navigate in this marketplace, first understand what buyers and lenders are looking for. Now, more than ever before, be prepared and put your company in the best possible light. We are not speaking about sales figures alone. In "Building a Better Box," we talked about many of the qualitative factors that make a business attractive to an external or internal buyer. Consider *all* of these factors and understand what your business is worth. Would you put your house on the market not knowing what price you should expect? No, and you would also estimate how much you would net after taxes and selling fees and the time it would take to bring it to market. You would enlist the best advisors you could find to give you good advice and assistance.

How much more important is the sale of your largest asset, your business? Yet, time and time again, people go to market with little forethought or preparation. No wonder there has been a dismal 80-percent failure rate!

Those owners who *are* successful in courting a qualified buyer are often shocked to find out the taxes and fees they will be facing. How do they continue to afford their lifestyles once the business is no longer providing income if they don't net enough from the sale?

Sadly, many of these things are not discussed and addressed until they are at the finish line, just before closing. Proper planning and sufficient time would have enabled the owner to address these issues, minimize the taxes and fees, and even "build a better box" to increase the value and cover their Wealth Gap.

Selling your business, whether to an individual, a competitor, a private equity group, or an individual investor is a potential minefield. You will need to continue to educate yourself and enlist the assistance of the right advisory team to build company value, prepare you to compete in the marketplace, perform pre-deal diligence, and address potential deal killers in advance ... all vital steps that are often overlooked.

TOP TEN DEAL KILLERS

Here is a summary of the most common mistakes that we have witnessed in the past several years while working with owners on more than 150 transactions:

1. **The owners do not understand how the business will be valued.** Most owners of closely held businesses have suppressed profits to reduce taxes. The company's financial statements do not begin to reflect the true value of the business. **The actual financial statements need to be restated to eliminate the owner's discretionary and non-recurring personal expenses, and attention drawn to off-balance-sheet assets, both tangible and intangible.**

2. **The owners have an unrealistic price in mind.** Recent surveys indicate that few companies have a current, accurate business valuation. Half of the time, owners are unrealistically high in their

asking price, and the other half of the time, they are low. **Whether you think your business is worth five million dollars or fifty million dollars, you need a professional opinion for reference purposes before you begin to discuss or justify a selling price that makes sense.**

3. **The owners do not understand the investor's motive.** Investors are looking to the future for return on investment and growth potential. The investor seldom buys what the seller thinks he is selling. **Owners would be wise to emphasize the business's growth potential rather than dwell on past performance.**

4. **The owners do not have proper counsel.** Talk with business owners who made an ill-fated attempt to sell their own business. Most wish they had used an experienced intermediary. **With professional help, you will get the right advice from those who have worked on a multitude of transactions.**

5. **The owners try to sell to the wrong people.** One of the biggest mistakes is to think that the best investor for the business is a competitor, customer, or supplier. If the deal does not happen, and most do not, then a great deal of confidential information about your company has been disclosed. Suddenly, everybody knows more about the company's profits and operations than they should. **Guard your information carefully and keep your intentions confidential unless you are ready to sell at a rock-bottom price.**

6. **The owners assume the best investor is local.** Most sellers naturally assume that the market for their business is the immediately surrounding area. However, thousands of very quiet private investment groups and offshore investors are interested in acquiring profitable, US based, privately held companies. **The world is now your marketplace, and the best investor may be anywhere across the country or around the world.**

7. **The company is not positioned for sale.** As we discussed in "Building a Better Box," organization, growth opportunity, reputation, and industry leadership are some of the many intangible qualities investors appreciate. **Documenting improvements that could be made by an investor with new capital helps you to position the company better and can increase value by 50 percent or more.**

8. **There is improper documentation.** Investors are evaluating the purchase based primarily on future growth potential and expected return on investment. They want to see what the profits would have looked like if you had run the business like a public company. They also want you to prepare three- to five-year pro forma financial projections, backed by solid market research substantiating the potential of the business. **Simply stated ... create a presentation to explain the past and sell the future.**

9. **The owners do not plan for the sale.** Many business owners have not calculated their Wealth

Gap or how much money they will need from the sale. Insisting on an all-cash deal, paid at closing, will result in savvy investors discounting their offering price by 35 percent or more! **Those who are willing to wait for some of the cash give the investor more flexibility to pay a higher price.**

10. **The owners are the first to mention price.** One cardinal rule of negotiating is never to be the first one at the table to mention price. An experienced acquirer who sees the potential may have a higher price in mind. As we know, value is very subjective. Owners will always regret leaving money on the table if they make this mistake. **Always let the prospective buyer be the first to mention price.**[1]

Don't make the same mistakes that these owners made …

I Want to Buy Your Business!

Music to a selling owner's ears! This well-established company had a strong foothold in its specialty retail space and was seeking a new owner. It had been in business for over twenty years, had a solid repeat-customer base, loyal employees, and a great sales history and projected future. It also had developed strong relationships with many suppliers over the years and had many high-end lines that competitors

---

1   Compiled in conjunction with Michael Nall, founder and president, Alliance of Merger and Acquisition Advisors, Chicago, Illinois.

wished they had but couldn't carry due to exclusive arrangements.

Even though these owners had engaged an intermediary to guide them in their sales effort, they felt that they could expedite the process since people approached them all of the time. What could it hurt to answer a few questions from people whom they knew? They would involve their advisor if and when the people inquiring actually proved to be serious about buying. After all, they would need their advisor to handle the paperwork.

Fast forward a few months. They called their advisor, with excitement in their voices, to say that they had someone very interested in the business and he was the perfect buyer. He had been one of their suppliers for years so he knew their business and the industry very well. Needless to say, the advisor had no idea that they had been speaking to this person, was alarmed, and asked some very important questions. Why had they not sent this candidate to the advisor to be screened? Had they given any confidential information to this person? Had they been discussing price or terms? The owners assured the advisor that this person was a trusted friend and there was no need to be concerned. Yes, they had given this potential buyer their tax returns and access to their records because they wanted to get the process moving. He was at their main location on a very regular basis anyway so it just made sense to speed the process up.

The advisor requested that this "buyer" contact him to sign the proper confidentiality agreements and have a discussion about his interest and financial capabilities to acquire the business. (By now, you may have figured out this is not going to have a happy ending.) The "buyer" had no intention of signing a confidentiality agreement that would restrict his ability to use the confidential information he had already received to compete against the seller.

It turns out that this "perfect buyer" did not have the financial resources or any genuine interest in acquiring the seller at all. Instead, he stole their customer lists, told their customers, employees, and suppliers that they were selling their company, and since he was in the industry, managed to maneuver the exclusive, lucrative product lines away from the owners to his new company. In essence, he stole their company right out from under them, and they willingly helped by feeding him the information he needed.

The ACTUAL Outcomes

- The sellers allowed themselves to be a target by being eager to sell and broadcasting that fact. They were excited that someone who seemed qualified was so interested in their company.

- They did not follow proper protocol and refer this "buyer" to their advisor, who could have vetted this individual and most likely protected them.

- The owners thought that the sales process was all about getting someone interested in their business and then just completing a bunch of paperwork to close the deal. They did not recognize the minefield they were stepping into until the bomb went off. They did not understand the "art of the deal."

- Ultimately, the owners lost their business, and even though they may have had the possibility of taking some type of civil action, they were too broke, tired, discouraged, and betrayed to fight. Their twenty years of hard work walked right out the door with their "friend."

- Both of the owners had to go find jobs in the industry, at age fifty-five, because they had no capital or desire to start over.

THE DESIRED OUTCOMES

- Hire the best advisors and heed their advice. If these owners had communicated their activities to their intermediary, he could have determined, very early on, if the potential buyer was a buyer at all. Buyers who will not sign a confidentiality agreement are not buyers. This is a real red flag. Chances are the "buyer" would have never even bothered to pursue or contact the intermediary since he was preying on the vulnerable by using his relationship and trust to gain access.

- Learn and understand how the deal process works and where the mines are buried so you don't take any missteps.

- Be prepared for the walk-in offer by knowing what your business is worth and how to manage the emotions that go along with this process.

- With the right planning and homework, these sellers could have sold their business to a real buyer and enjoyed their retirement as they had envisioned.

Advisory Teams

The importance of having the right people on your advisory team cannot be stressed enough. Understanding the motivation and collaborative abilities of all team members is crucial to your ultimate success. Make sure *your* goals and objectives are "top of mind" for all advisors and you are receiving assistance accordingly. Be sure to have a deal quarterback who can manage the process effectively … you will need and appreciate the assistance.

~

Selling your business is usually a once-in-a-lifetime opportunity. Make it a successful one!

~

Conclusion

Paint by Numbers

Just as numbers on a canvas guide you to paint in the shapes with the proper colors, this ownership-transition planning process will enable you to put a plan in place to achieve your goals and move successfully to the next phase of your life. The plan will ultimately be your own transition masterpiece.

～

A Business Ownership Transition Plan is a comprehensive written document that outlines how and when the ownership of a business will be transferred to others, either internally or externally, in order to achieve the owner's goals.

～

THE PLANNING PROCESS

In "Getting Yourself Prepared," we outlined both financial and non-financial goals that you may have for your business-ownership transition. Once you have identified your goals, you will use them in "Follow the Yellow Brick Road" and "The Art of the Deal" to see how well they match to the different transition options.

In "Counting Beans," we discussed taking stock of what you have saved outside your business, your post-transition income needs, and how to calculate your Wealth Gap, or how much money will be needed from the transition to meet your income needs.

In "Building a Better Box," we discussed how businesses are valued and some key drivers of that value. You will use your estimated business value to determine how much money you will likely net from the different transition options in "The Art of the Deal." You will then compare these net figures to the Wealth Gap you calculated above to determine which transition strategies will close your gap and provide the money that you will need post-transition.

If none of the transition options net you enough money to meet your financial needs today, you can take action to bridge the gap before you transition the ownership of your business. Multiple ways exist to close the gap and some of these include:

- Saving more money outside the business
- Increasing the value of your company
- Decreasing your spending and income needs
- Developing additional sources of post-transition income

REVIEW OF KEY CONCEPTS

Getting Yourself Prepared

- Preparing yourself for transition is the first and most important step in this process.

- Your identity may now be one with your business, and it will take time to separate the two.

- Consider both financial and non-financial goals when you think about ownership transition.

- We all have multiple facets to our lives. Consider each one as you develop your transition goals and architect your life plan.

- It will be very important for you to identify your fears, concerns, and other barriers that may impede your planning efforts so they can be addressed early in the process.

Counting Beans

- Counting beans involves taking stock of the assets you have saved outside of the business, calculating how much income you will need post-transition, and then determining how much money you will need to net from the ownership transition, also known as the Wealth Gap.

- Counting your beans will allow you to assess how financially dependent you are on the business.

- Owners often make the mistake of ratcheting up their lifestyles to match the increasing company profits instead of saving money outside to diversify their holdings and reduce their risks.

- Saving significant money outside the business not only reduces the Wealth Gap but also gives the owner more transition options. For example, he may be able to afford to sell the business to his children or key managers instead of an outside buyer.

- Every owner needs a contingency plan, regardless of age or desire for an ownership transition. You never know when a life event may occur.

Building a Better Box

- Most owners have not saved enough money outside their businesses and will therefore need the wealth trapped inside their company to fund their next phases of life.

- All businesses are inherently risky, no matter how long they have been in existence.

- Remain vigilant, continue to innovate, and learn how to maximize the value of your business.

- Privately held companies have a range of values. Each prospective buyer will determine how much he is willing to pay, based on his perceived risk, as well as the normalized earnings and quality of the business.

- Many, many qualitative factors drive business value, including: predictable and increasing revenue and profits, clean financials, solid management team to avoid dependence on the owner, quality products and services, strong sales and marketing, low risk, and systems and processes for running the business.

Follow the Yellow Brick Road

- Two general types of ownership transition options exist—internal and external. "Internal" refers to selling or gifting the business to insiders, such as key employees, managers, or family members involved in the business. "External" refers to selling to an outsider, such as a competitor, customer, or investor.

- Each transition option has its own transfer value, associated taxes, and fees, as well as pros and cons. Our planning process allows you to assess each option and determine how well it meets both your financial and non-financial goals.

- Selling externally may not net you the most money, even if the gross selling price is the highest, so it is important to do the math. Internal transitions often can be structured in a tax-efficient manner.

- If owners plan ahead, they will typically have more options from which to choose.

- Selling as a last resort, due to a life event, will typically net you the least amount of money.

- No matter which transition option is chosen, it will be very important for owners to delegate duties and relinquish some control so the business may run without them. This will increase the value of the business, ensure its continuity, and make it more appealing to buyers.

Art of the Deal

- Selling externally is desired by many owners, but of those who make an attempt, less than one in five actually consummate a transaction.

- The business-transfer/merger-and-acquisition (M&A) market for privately held businesses runs in cycles that sometimes favor buyers and, at other times, sellers.

- Understand the business-transfer marketplace to achieve the best possible results. It is unwise to simply pick a target age for the transition without regard to what is occurring in the marketplace.

- The art is in positioning the business, finding the right buyer, and negotiating the best possible deal.

- Baby-boomer business owners will be flooding the market in the next ten to fifteen years as they attempt to transition their businesses to others. This is likely to drive business values down.

- Planning well in advance will dramatically improve your chances of selling to an outsider at a desirable price.

- Know what your business is worth, what advisory fees will have to be paid, and how the transaction will be taxed in order to maximize your net proceeds, regardless of which transition option is chosen.

- The selling process is a minefield, and you will definitely need assistance to navigate it successfully and avoid deal killers.

- Choose advisors who respect your goals, collaborate well with others, and are well versed in business-ownership transitions.

What happens when you use this process and pull all of these pieces together into a comprehensive plan? Meet Roger …

The Deal of a Lifetime

Roger had just turned seventy years young when we met in late 2010, and his recent birthday had triggered some thoughts about life beyond the business. Roger was in very good health, and he was still very active and passionate about the business that he had started more than three decades earlier. He was a skillful CEO and tremendous salesperson and had grown his company to over fifty million dollars in revenue by personally closing a multitude of multi-million-dollar, long-term contracts. The company's primary business was providing educational services to at-risk youth that enabled them to graduate from high school and put their lives on a more promising path.

Roger had a loyal management team who were in their fifties and sixties, and they were anxious to know what would happen to the company if Roger was unable to continue at the helm. Roger had implemented a leadership development program for some of the young stars in the company, but he had not groomed anyone to take over and thus had no real succession plan. A strategic buyer had approached Roger annually for the last several years when Roger did not yet have a plan, but he was just not ready to think about life beyond the business.

We worked with Roger to discuss his life beyond the company, document his goals, assess his financial dependence on the transition, determine a likely range of values for the company, and analyze which transition options were best suited to his needs—all key components of his Business Ownership Transition Plan.

Our analysis showed that selling to an outside buyer was the option that was most likely to achieve all of Roger's goals. He had always focused on the company's mission of helping others and reinvesting profits back into the company. Roger never took a substantial amount of money out of the company for his own personal use.

It was important to Roger that his management team have a "soft landing," regardless of which transition strategy was chosen. The management team approached Roger with their desire to purchase the company, and Roger gave thoughtful consideration to their plan, even though they could not come close to matching the prospective buyer's offer. The management team was unable to secure the necessary financing, and a few team members began thinking about their own retirement in the near future. Ultimately, they decided that purchasing the company was just not feasible.

We assembled and coordinated the deal team, and discussions began in earnest with the strategic buyer that had previously approached Roger for the last several years. This time Roger had a plan, and he was ready to think about life beyond the business. Nine months later, Roger closed on the largest deal of his life—the sale of his company for more money than he ever believed possible—the deal of a lifetime!

This deal enabled Roger to achieve his own personal financial goals, which included setting aside money for his heirs and leaving substantial gifts to two educational institutions that were instrumental in giving him his good start in life. He was also able to provide special bonuses to his loyal management team and severance pay for the small percentage of employees who would not be staying on with the buyer.

Developing a transition plan in advance of the sale allowed Roger to achieve his goals, realize a huge tax savings, and financially secure his future. It also enabled him to begin to separate himself from the business, envision his life post-transition, and get ready to move on before the deal was closed.

Roger is currently finishing up his one-year, post-sale consulting contract with the buyer, and letting go has been somewhat difficult at times, but he is adjusting well to his new life and really enjoying more travel, golf, and his volunteer work with at-risk youth. He has not lost his passion, but now, he is passionate about creating and really *living* his new life and having the freedom to do what he wants to do. We have encouraged Roger to think about writing a book and doing some motivational speaking as well. His passion, wisdom, and experience are tremendous and would be appreciated and enjoyed by others.

Roger worked hard and shouldered all of the risk as he built a valuable company that saved thousands of kids and provided jobs for thousands of employees for over thirty years—quite a legacy, *and* the mission continues today under the new owner.

All owners, regardless of business size need to plan for their ownership transitions well in advance. This is particularly important for owners who are very dependent on their businesses for their financial security.

Don't wait for something to rock YOUR world. With proper planning, you will have more control over your future and have a much better chance of achieving your goals and closing YOUR last great deal!

~

We encourage you to visit our website, www.BusinessTransitionAcademy.com, to continue your education on this important topic. If you purchased this book as part of a training course, please complete the workbook and online forms to create your own custom ownership-transition plan.

~

ABOUT THE AUTHORS

JANE M. JOHNSON

As a former business owner who successfully guided her business for fourteen years until it was acquired in 2004, **Jane M. Johnson** discovered how much time, planning, and preparation were necessary in order to achieve her personal goals and ensure the continuity of her business.

Jane spent the early part of her career in public accounting and finance at General Electric, and she became inspired to start her own business after becoming a certified public accountant (CPA) in 1990. Her mission was to teach business owners how to improve their operations and boost the value of their companies by leveraging technology and business-process optimization. Jane's team developed an outstanding reputation by providing exceptional software products and consulting services to more than 350 mid-market clients in an array of industries across New England. Jane believes that her ten-year

Vistage membership was instrumental to her success in building her firm's value.

After finding a lack of objective transition advisors in the marketplace, Jane forged ahead on her own. She maximized the value of her firm and then negotiated the sale, retaining 100 percent of her clients and team members in the process. She spent the next three years as a partner in the buyer's firm, driving continual growth in revenue from both products and services. This eye-opening experience fueled her desire to assist other business owners with their ownership transitions.

After leaving the buyer in 2007, Jane became a certified business exit consultant (CBEC), a certified merger and acquisition advisor (CM&AA), and a professional family business advisor (FBA) to further her education in the field of ownership-transition planning. In 2010, she received the Excellence in Exit Planning Achievement Award from Pinnacle Equity Solutions for her highly regarded services to business owners seeking successful ownership transitions. Today, as an independent and objective advisor, Jane remains passionate about teaching and assisting other business owners with maximizing company value and achieving all of their ownership-transition goals.

Jane enjoys teaching, writing, spending time with her family, hiking, biking, skiing, TRX, and yoga.

KATHLEEN RICHARDSON-MAURO

Kathleen Richardson-Mauro has owned and operated five small companies in thirty-plus years, and she has successfully assisted over 150 small business owners in identifying and achieving their business-transition goals. As an entrepreneur herself, she has a personal understanding of business-ownership challenges and can empathize with the business owner.

Her professional career began in the banking industry in the 1970s, and she later worked in different capacities within the accounting profession. Her passion for helping people led her to enter financial planning, and in 1992, she became a certified financial planner (CFP) and opened a fee-only financial planning firm as a registered investment advisor (RIA) with a focus on estate planning. In early 2000, she entered the field of mergers and acquisitions, utilizing the combination of her professional experiences. Her passion for assisting people evolved further in 2007 by broadening her focus from the purely transactional world to the field of planning business-ownership transitions.

Kathleen's passion for assisting the owners of privately held businesses continues today. Her goal is to help them determine, plan, and execute their own successful exit strategies, allowing them to live life on their terms. She works alongside business owners who are searching for unbiased assistance in determining which transition strategies will meet their individual needs. By being highly educated and experienced in this emerging profession, she guides business owners in successfully planning these business transitions while maximizing the wealth that is trapped in, most likely, their largest asset. Her unique background and skill set enable her to assist the owners in a holistic and client-centered manner that not only considers all of the complex financial aspects of comprehensive transition planning but also takes into consideration the often-overlooked personal preparation that is required for a successful transition.

Kathleen is a graduate of the College of Financial Planning in Denver, CO, a certified merger and acquisition advisor (CM&AA), a professional family business advisor (FBA), a certified business intermediary (CBI), and a certified business exit consultant (CBEC). Most recently, she served on the certification committee for the development of the CBEC program, and she will serve on the Alliance of Mergers & Acquisition Advisors Education Committee in 2013.

Kathleen is active in her community and her church, and she enjoys spending time with her family, being outdoors, traveling, sailing, hiking, and playing golf.